GENEVA
INTERNATIONAL

Copyright © 1995 Pyramid Media Group

ISBN I-85310-700-X
British Library Cataloging-in-Publication Data
A catalog record for this book is available from the British
Library.

First published in UK in 1995 by
Airlife Publishing Ltd.

Text by Aram Gesar
Foreword and introduction by Geneva Airport
Edited by Michael O. Lavitt

All photographs:
Copyright © 1977-95 Aram Gesar
Except on pages:
J.-L. Altherr: 18, 40, 41, 47, 51-55, 57, 59, 61-66, 68-75, 78-81, 83,
85-87, 89-105, 107-117.
Geneva Airport: 4, 6-12, 108, 118.

A Book edited and produced for Airlife by
Pyramid Media Group
29, route de Pré-Bois
CH-1215 Geneva Airport
Switzerland

Printed and bound in Italy

Airlife Publishing Ltd.
101 Longden Road, Shrewsbury, England SY3 9EB

GENEVA
INTERNATIONAL
AIRPORT

Aram Gesar

AUTHOR'S NOTE

Geneva airport is a very special place for me. My first encounters with aircraft and airports started in Geneva. Growing up in this town I saw my first aircraft and flew for the first time here. My first flight was on a Fokker F27-100, and the second on a Vickers Viscount during the late 1950s. With the advent of the first jets in the region, I saw, from the observation deck of the old terminal building, my first turbojet-powered aircraft, an Air France "Caravelle" on the Paris Orly-Geneva run in the fall of 1959.

I experienced my first jet flights in the early 1960s on Swissair's exciting and very fast Convair 990, the Caravelle 3 and eventually the DC-8 and 707, along with short range flights in piston and turboprop aircraft such as the Convair 440 "Metropolitan" and Lockheed L-188 Electras.

Cointrin inaugurated the new terminal with its underground tunnels to the satellites in 1968, just in time for the advent of the wide bodies. The first 747 arrived in early 1970 for a visit and dwarfed all other aircraft parked near it. Regular operations followed in 1971 followed by the DC-10 and L-1011 trijets.

Flying frequently in and out of Geneva is a delight: it takes less than 30 minutes to get to the airport and the check-in and boarding are delightfully short. Having lived the last twenty years in New York, where airport access is difficult, this is a welcome change.

During the preparation of this book, I have been fortunate to receive help and advice from people associated with Geneva's Cointrin airport. I thank everyone who has answered our requests for access to the airport, aircraft and information so patiently. Everyone I came into contact with was most helpful, but I would particularly like to express my gratitude to Jean-Pierre Jobin, Pierre Germain, Philippe Roy, Daniel Teysseire, and flight crews and ground personnel of Balair, British Airways, and Swissair.

Aram Gesar

FOREWORD

On January 1, 1994, Genève-Cointrin Airport became Geneva International Airport (AIG). Was this merely a change of name? Far from it, for on the very same day, 74 years after its creation, the airport officially acquired a new status which will enable it to better meet the challenges of the closing years of the century.

Prior to 1994, Geneva Airport had been an integral part of the Department of Public Economy of the Republic and Canton of Geneva. Because of this, any decisions involving major investments had to be taken by the Geneva parliament. Political uncertainties adversely affected the airport and curbed its smooth development.

The benefits of the new status, which granted financial autonomy to the government-owned corporation of Geneva International Airport, quickly showed themselves. In May 1994, the airport's Board of Directors decided to equip two central satellites, which are located directly on the tarmac, with telescopic gangways. These will offer greatly improved passenger comfort and safety.

Current extension work on the airport, aimed at practically doubling the terminal's surface area and increasing passenger capacity to eight million a year, is due to be completed by the beginning of 1996. Meanwhile, the Board of Directors has to decide upon the updating of the existing installations: the next step needs to be the creation of new boarding lounges, and a new Y-shaped satellite building linked to the current terminal by an automatic shuttle system.

Equally as important as the improvement of the airport's infrastructure is the reinforcement of its air links. Geneva International Airport boasts, thanks particularly to Swissair, an extremely good network of short- and medium-haul links that few similar cities in Europe can claim to equal. However, there is a weak point concerning the airport's intercontinental links.

Although the airport's "catchment" area has a population of only two million, it is the scene of intense activity, both economic and, thanks to the presence in Geneva of all the many international organisations, political. So we can see that there is a significant growth potential for direct long-haul routes to both South America and, above all, the Far East. In order to capitalise on this potential, the management of AIG has launched an unprecedented marketing campaign, and all the indications are that this will bear fruit.

Thus, with more than 5,000 people working on the airport site, and with its excellent motorway and rail links, Geneva International Airport will be better and better able to serve as the "lungs" of a whole region astride three countries: Switzerland, France and Italy.

Jean-Pierre JOBIN, Director General

A SHORT HISTORY OF GENEVA AIRPORT

It was in 1909 - the year of Louis Blériot's first transatlantic crossing - that the first flight trials took place in the Geneva region. The Dufaux brothers, Armand and Henri, who had built their own monoplane, made several attempts in Viry (Haute-Savoie), on the other side of the French border. However, their greatest feat was accomplished on Aug. 28, 1910, when Armand Dufaux left from Noville (on the extreme eastern side of Lake Geneva) and landed in La Gabiule, near Geneva, having thus covered 85 km along the lake in 56 minutes. He thereby also pocketed the 5,000-franc prize money offered by the Genevan firm Perrot-Duval to reward the first pilot to cross Lake Geneva at its longest stretch without flying over land.

While World War I was to temporarily curb development of aviation in Geneva's skies, the progress achieved by the "flying machines" was to prove tremendous. François Durafour, before his historic landing atop Mont Blanc, had already begun to offer passenger flights from a small site in Saint-Georges on the northwestern outskirts of Geneva.

This site was nonetheless much too small to allow for commercial activity. In October 1919, the Grand Conseil voted a law declaring "state approval for the acquisition of the real estate necessary for the creation of an airfield with a surface area of around 137 hectares, on the territory of Collex, Bellevue, Genthod and Versoix communes". While specifying that nothing over eight meters high could be built or planted on a 150-meter-wide strip bordering the future land, the deputies allocated a 650,000-franc budget for the acquisition and establishment of an aviation field.

In actual fact, this law was modified and, on June 19, 1920, another site was selected near the villages of Meyrin and Cointrin, some 4 km north of the town. The location was good, as the proximity of the Jura mountain ranges and of the Salève ensured a fairly stable régime of dominant

winds, namely the northeasterly bise and its southeasterly counterpart.

Under these circumstances, it was possible to build a single runway, a situation still prevailing today. The land had a surface area of 575,000 square meters and was around 1 km long with a minimum width of 430 meters.

Cointrin airport was officially and legally "born" on Sept. 22, 1920, by virtue of the operating permission granted by the Federal Aviation Authority, and the official inauguration of the land was marked on Sept. 23 at 10.20 am, by the landing of military pilot Edgar Primault at the controls of a Swiss-made Haefeli D.H. 3 aircraft.

However, it was only in 1922 that the first commercial flights actually began. The first routes opened were Geneva-Lausanne-Paris, Geneva-Lyon and Geneva-Zurich-Munich-Nuremberg.

At that time, the aerodrome was comparatively modest, spread over a turfed area of 24 hectares (compared with 320 hectares today, corresponding to 1% of the canton's total surface area) and consisted of a small, two-floor administrative building housing a refreshment stand and two wooden hangars able to shelter a dozen or so planes. Nonetheless, its radio equipment included two 30-meter high masts and, even more importantly, a radiogoniometer (direction finder) able to guide planes. The whole complex was inaugurated on May 21, 1922 by a military aviation show involving 18 aircraft.

Subsequently, orders came to build more permanent structures. From 1926 to 1931, the wooden hangars were replaced by brickwork buildings, covered with a metal framework. They were relatively large for the times, as they featured a 40-meter opening and a depth of some 30 meters.

In 1937 the real revolution took place with the construction of a concrete runway, 405 meters long and 21 meters wide. It was linked by tarmac taxiways to the parking platform in front of the hangars. This represented a first in Switzerland.

Simultaneously, it became necessary to move the two antenna-bearing pylons which were an obstacle to aerial navigation. They were set up 1.5 km to the south of the airfield.

By the end of the thirties, it became obvious that air transport would undergo rapid development, using ever larger aircraft and therefore necessitating a corresponding adaptation of installations. In 1940, the Genevan authorities adopted a modernization plan making provision for a 1,065-meter-long concrete runway, enlargement of the parking area, installation of a lighting system for the field, a new network of radio-electric equipment and the construction of a new air terminal.

The war was to put a halt to the implementation of this program, although not for long. The authorities had become aware that the technical progress being made by aircraft construction companies meant that planes were becoming increasingly heavy. Exceptionally large-scale work for the time - particularly in a wartime period - was therefore undertaken with the help of the Confederation.

The concrete runway was extended to 2,000 meters, and the total site now spread over 210 hectares. These installations, unique in Switzerland, were to make it possible - right from the end of hostilities - to link Geneva to the largest European cities and even to the United States. It was thus that, in May 1947, flight commander Walter Borner flew a Swissair DC-4 from Geneva to New York and back.

The modernization process was accelerated over the following years: in 1948, a large hangar was brought into service and in 1949, an air terminal at last worthy of the name became operational. The latter had been designed for a passenger flow of 300,000, and experts estimated that it would take at least ten years to reach that number. There were in fact 208,841 as early as 1950 - the first year of use - and as many as 468,329 five years later; the million mark was reached in 1962.

By the mid-fifties, the forthcoming arrival of commercial jets was becoming increasingly probable, with all that it would entail: the necessity of longer runways and increased capacity of the air terminal. The Genevan authorities, who had owned and operated the airport right from its beginnings, submitted a new modernization programme to the Grand Conseil. At the end of 1956, the parliament approved the necessary budgetary allocations, and in the following year the Federal Council in turn presented an expansion program for the two Swiss airports catering to intercontinental traffic, Geneva-Cointrin and Zurich-Kloten.

For Geneva, the first problem was that of extending the runway, which had already been increased to 2,600 meters in 1953, but which now needed to be adapted to the requirements of jet planes. The best solution was clearly an extension to the northeast, on French territory. It was thus necessary to proceed to an exchange of territory with France.

An agreement on this matter was negotiated and also provided for reserving a sector of the future air terminal as a "French airport", linked to France via the city of Ferney-Voltaire by a tax-free route. This agreement was ratified by the Federal Assembly in 1956 and by the French Parliament in 1958. Work on extending the runway took just under two years, bringing it to a total length of 3,900 meters. Construction of the new air terminal was undertaken in 1962. During the same period, a road tunnel, three satellites in the middle of the tarmac accessible by underpasses, a Swissair hotel center and new radioelectric installations were also built.

Inaugurated by the cantonal and federal authorities on May 17, 1968 , the new air terminal was referred to at the time as the most modern in Europe. It had been designed to handle five million passengers per year, and although the arrival of jumbo jets was already foreseen - the first TWA Boeing 747 made a demonstration landing in 1970 - this capacity was deemed to be sufficient up until the year 2000.

This optimism was soon belied by the facts. During its first full operational year in 1969, the new terminal witnessed a passenger flow of 2.5 million. The five million mark was reached in 1985, and it then became obvious that a new adaptation program was needed. In that same year, the "Horizon 90" strategy was announced, aimed at creating a 7-million passenger capacity by 1990.

Work was to involve both the town side of the airport - with an extension of the air terminal, providing greater capacity on departure and arrival levels - and on the tarmac side with the building of a Y satellite able to cater to jumbo jets and linked to the central air terminal by an automatic shuttle system. A new baggage sorting system was also foreseen, as was a railway station putting Cointrin only six minutes from the town-center and offering access to all major

railway lines arriving in Geneva. CFF, the Swiss Railway system, managed and funded the latter project.

Political ups and downs were in fact to modify and above all delay the program. While priority had been given to the work on the tarmac side, it was in fact on the town side that things finally got underway.

Changes were to include the complete overhaul of the arrivals hall, linked to the operational startup of the CFF railway station on May 31, 1987; modernization of the departure hall, with new baggage registration counters and an enlarged and renovated shopping mezzanine; and the construction of a new baggage sorting system, on which Swissair built its new centre, which also houses the International Air Transport Association headquarters.

A freight hall, capable of handling 100,000 tonnes per year, was built to the east of the air terminal. It became operational on May 31, 1988.

This effort to adapt to new demands is far from over. Currently the extension of the main air terminal is nearing completion; it will increase the capacity of arrival and departure zones with new registration counters enabling more airlines to provide "self check-in" facilities. Above all, it will make procedures run more smoothly for passengers on busy days. This zone, which will be operational at the beginning of 1996, was preceded by complete reorganization of the restaurant system.

The next stage will involve equipping two of the satellites with telescopic gangways, which will enhance passenger comfort. This equipment, to be installed in 1995, is one of the first fruits of the new status acquired by the airport January 1, 1994.

With the entry into force of this status, the airport no longer receives state budgetary allocations, but is free to decide on its in-vestments and to finance them either by its own resources or by borrowing.

The "Etablissement Public Autonome Aéroport International de Genève" is managed by a 19-member Board of Directors. Seven of them - including the president - are appointed by the State Council. Two are representatives of airport users, including one from Swissair. The other members are designated as follows: five by the Grand Conseil, two by staff, two by bordering towns (Meyrin and Grand-Saconnex), two by "cantons" within French-speaking Switzerland, and one by the Ain and Haute-Savoie French "départements".

The director general of the airport takes part in the proceedings of the Board of Directors with a consultative voice. Within the Board of Directors, a five-member Management Committee is responsible for day-to-day management of the "Etablissement".

Checking-in on a busy winter day can become a hassle. The airport is improving and modernizing equipment and facilities to speed up the process.

The airport's new train station allows rapid transit to Geneva, other Swiss towns and most major European cities.

Flag carrier Swissair flies a fleet of McDonnell Douglas MD-81s, MD-11s, Airbus A310s, Fokker 100s and Boeing 747s. One of Geneva's three airside satellite terminals is at right, while the main terminal rises in the background.

◀ Geneva's satellite terminals will soon have motorized boarding ramps as found in many newer airports. For passengers who love to fly, walking out onto the apron and boarding via airstairs can be a thrill in itself. It brings them closer to the flight line, recalling the days when getting close to the action was routine. Walking through a boarding ramp is convenient in bad weather, but also accentuates the sterility of many modern airports.

▲ Passengers deplane from an MD-81 while catering trucks provide meals for the next group of passengers. A pair of Pratt & Whitney JT8D engines, each rated at 8,732 kg. (19,250 lb.), powers the "Mad Dog." This aircraft is configured with an internal set of airstairs.

A British Airways 737-200 taking off. The airline flies this type between Geneva and the UK cities of London and Manchester. British Airways is the second largest international user of Geneva airport, and has had a significant influence on its expansion. Also, the airline's links with the airport go back a very long way, as one of its forerunners was one of the first international carriers to use the airport.

Air France uses Fokker F28s on most of its flights between
Nice and Geneva.

Though battered by huge losses in the early 1990s, United Airlines grew under deregulation in the United States, buying many international routes from competitors who fared less well. ▼

The seventh MD-11 (HB-IWH) of Swissair gets ready to ▶ enter Runway 23 for its takeoff roll and flight to New York's Kennedy airport. The flight used to be serviced by 747-300s inbound from Zurich continuing to JFK. The airline chose Pratt & Whitney PW4460 engines to power its McDonnell Douglas MD-11s.

British Airways used A320 aircraft for its Gatwick-Geneva
link for some years, but now mainly uses Boeing 737s.

Crossair is the little sister of Swissair. It uses smaller aircraft like this turboprop-powered Fokker 50, Saab 340 and 2000, BAe 146 and RJ85 to fly shorter routes with fewer passengers, who then can connect with longer flights on DC-10-30s or other large intercontinental airliners.

The Apron Management System is built atop the main terminal building and is used to direct aircraft traffic on the tarmac and taxiways.

The MD-81s in service with Swissair since 1980 are powered by two Pratt & Whitney JT8D-217Cs with a maximum takeoff weight of about 64,000 kg. (141,100 lb.). They will all be replaced as of 1995 by Airbus A319, A320 and A321 aircraft.

Special service vehicles can be seen on the tarmac near the main terminal building. The airport has a very good special passenger and VIP handling service. Great attention is given to passengers with special requests and to international dignitaries.

A Swissair MD-81 and an SAS DC-9-41 are parked at their gates of the round satellites. The latter airline flies to Geneva several times a day from Scandinavia. Many airlines, scheduled and charter alike, prefer to fly only a single aircraft type. This cuts training costs in all areas, as well as making maintenance more efficient.

Sabena operates 737 and BAe 146 aircraft on its Brussels-
Geneva route.

A Novair DC-10-30.

A Swissair MD-11 rotates for takeoff. The airline started to operate the aircraft in 1991 to replace its fleet of DC-10-30s. The McDonnell Douglas MD-11 airliner is certificated as a derivative of the DC-10 trijet. The new fuselage is about 6 meters (20 feet) longer, allowing as many as 30 extra passengers. The MD-11 is offered with engines from two manufacturers and has a "glass" cockpit in which cathode ray tubes replace traditional instruments. The most apparent difference from the DC-10 is the MD-11's winglets.

A Boeing 737-200 of Sabena prepares to start its journey departing from one of the airside satellite terminals. Only 30 aircraft were built in the original Model 737-100 configuration, this version quickly being superseded by the Model 737-200, with a fuselage stretch of 1.82 meters (6 feet) to allow basic accommodation for 119 and, eventually, a maximum of 130. United Airlines was the first to order this variant, and the fifth example of the Model 737 to fly, on Aug. 8, 1967, was the first stretched Model 737-200.

▲ A Fokker 100 on approach to Runway 23. HB-IVG is the seventh 100 delivered to Swissair, the launch customer. It is an improved version of the very popular F28, and is powered by the very quiet Rolls-Royce Tay 620-15 powerplants.

Iran Air is one of the few ▶ operators flying 747s to Geneva. The Boeing 747SP is optimized for range. It carries fewer passengers but more fuel than other members of the 747 family, giving it a maximum range of 12,300 km. (7,670 mi.). Only the newest 747, the -400, can fly farther.

A United Airlines 727-200, formerly a Pan Am Eurohub aircraft, is serviced before takeoff, while an Airbus A310 taxis nearby. United has embarked on one of the boldest experiments in aviation history. The airline's workers bought a controlling interest in the carrier in a deal valued at $4.9 billion. In return for financing, they are making concessions in pay, benefits and work rules.

Winglets like those on the MD-11 provide additional lift. Swissair has a long relationship with McDonnell Douglas. It launched or co-launched the DC-9-30, -50, -80 (MD-80), DC-10-30 and MD-11. It was one of the first airlines to acquire DC-9-15s in the 1960s. In September 1980, the carrier received its first MD-81.

◀ Saudi Arabian Airlines wants to replace its L-1011-200 Tri-Stars with new technology aircraft. Its long-range fleet also has 747-100, -200 and -300 aircraft. Saudia placed big orders with Boeing and McDonnell Douglas in 1993, but Airbus Industrie vowed to fight for a piece of the pie.

The 737 and the Fokker 100 are ▶ the only types of aircraft KLM operates on its flights between Amsterdam and Geneva.

The British Aerospace 146-200 used to be available in three versions: all passenger, all cargo and convertible. Now all have been replaced by the Avro RJ70, 85, 100 and 115. Apron parking is necessary to open up valuable gate space at Geneva.

The DC-10's cargo holds have a total volume of 130 cubic meters (4,618 cubic feet.), and the new MD-11 can even carry 20 percent more. Passengers often don't think about it, but air cargo is a key component of virtually every airline's business. In the background stands the Swissair Center and IATA's European headquarters.

▲ An Avro RJ85 on final approach to Runway 05 in Crossair's new, exciting livery. Crossair's old livery made its association with Swissair more apparent.

Airbus Industrie's A320 is truly a multinational aircraft. ▶ The aircraft is assembled in Toulouse, France, using components built by the European consortium's partners in Britain, France, Germany, Italy and Spain. The initial choice of engines was between the CFM56-5, produced by the General Electric/Snecma partnership under the CFM International marketing organization, and the V2500 produced by the International Aero Engines consortium.

The Convair CV440 is still operated by smaller airlines carrying cargo and passengers. Swissair operated this aircraft in the passenger version for flights between Geneva and Zurich during the 1950s and 60s, until it was replaced by DC-9 service.

The Saab SF-340B is still a reliable turboprop for short-haul
routes. It can carry 35 passengers and cruises at 285 knots
(527 kph., 327 mph.).

Trans World Airlines took a severe beating in the late ▶ 1980s and early 1990s as it underwent two ownership changes and a bankruptcy. Nevertheless, it pioneered the concept of long, overwater flights of twinjets. So-called ETOPS (extended-range twin-engine operations over water) flights would not be possible without the advanced systems of planes like the Boeing 767. The airline no longer flies to Geneva.

▲ The newest Boeing 737 in the sky is the -500, a smaller version of the new technology members of the family. The -300, -400 and -500 all use CFM 56-series engines, made by a consortium of General Electric and Snecma of France. Earlier 737s use Pratt & Whitney engines.

The Boeing 747SP was designed with the long-haul Pacific market in mind. It can fly from there to Europe or the United States without stopping to refuel. The aircraft was a shortened version of the 747-100 for very long operations such as New York to Tokyo. It started non-stop service on that route in 1975. Only about 44 of the 1,000 747s in service are the short-body 747SP. Air Mauritius now flies an A340 aircraft to Geneva.

Air Algeria flies an extensive route network in Europe and the Middle East. The bulk of its fleet is composed of Boeing 737-200s like this one and older 727-200s.

Ground controllers have a tricky job coordinating the movement of large and small aircraft around the tarmac of a major international airport like Geneva. Pilots must learn a whole set of "rules of the road" for navigating on the ground, as well as in the air.

Although not the first jetliner, the Boeing 707 was the first one considered a commercial success. The dawn of the jet age coincides with the 707's debut in 1958 in the colors of Pan American World Airways. Boeing built 9l7 Model 707s (excluding airframes for the E-3 and E-6 military programs), made up of 63 -120, 78 -120B, five -220, 69 -320, 174 -320B (shown here), 337 -320C, 37 -420, 65 -720 and 89 -720B variants.

Switzerland's friendly banking laws and historic neutrality help draw business people and diplomats from the Middle East and elsewhere, while the Alps attract those who are looking for the thrill of flying down a mountain on skis.

British Airways' European fleet includes 737-200, -300 and -400 aircraft.

▲ A Dassault Falcon is parked near the general aviation tarmac on the north side of the airport where the grass strip Runway 05/23 is also located.

◀ The weather observation station near the threshold of Runway 23 can be seen.

The thrill of flying begins as the wheels leave the runway and the nose points skyward. The aircraft taking off is a McDonnell Douglas MD-80. Pilots say it handles like a jet fighter. Passengers flying in airliners like the MD-80 series and DC-9 enjoy a quieter ride because the engines are mounted in the rear.

A former Swissair CV990A. Howard Hughes, the late, eccentric billionaire, designed the Convair 990 in the late 1950s. The sleek aircraft flew close to the speed of sound in tests, but appearance and performance were not enough to guarantee success. The 990 was certified in late 1961, but the program was killed a little more than two years later.

Pan American World Airways flew Airbus A310s on European routes before collapsing. Delta Air Lines bought many of its route authorities and aircraft.

This Fokker 100 prototype lists some of the initial customers for the medium-range twinjet. The Fokker 100 is a favorite of airlines flying short to medium-haul routes. It offers a high-tech "glass" cockpit, fuel efficient operation from rugged Rolls-Royce Tay 620 turbofan engines and meets stringent Stage 3 or Class 3 noise regulations.

◀ A CTA Caravelle is about to cross the threshold of Runway 05. Geneva Airport is just 4 km. (2.5 miles) north of the city's center, making it convenient for travelers arriving by auto or train. It has a single concrete Runway 05/23.

◀ A Swissair 747-357 prepares to land at Geneva. The snow-capped Jura mountains offer a picturesque background. Boeing formally launched the Model 747-300 on the basis of an order from Swissair that included both passenger and -300M Combi versions. The latter has a side-loading freight door. The first -300 flew on Oct. 5, 1982, with Pratt and Whitney JT9D-7R4G2 engines, and the second on Dec. 10, 1982, with General Electric CF6-50E2 engines.

A Finnair DC-9-30 is serviced near the main terminal. This type is designed for medium-haul journeys with a maximum range of 2,150 km. (1,340 miles). Finnair also operates the MD-11.

CTA now operates the MD-87, replacing the Caravelles.

The first twinjet, the French-built Sud-Est Aviation Caravelle, was a pioneer in the late 1950s. But U.S. manufacturers Boeing and Douglas Aircraft Co. dominated the market until Airbus Industrie became a major player in the 1980s.

◀ Lufthansa flies mostly a mix of 737-200s, -300s and -400s to Geneva, with a few A320s.

The DC-8 is still popular with charter operators, although few remain in scheduled service today. Most used Pratt & Whitney engines, although the Series 40 was equipped with four Rolls-Royce powerplants. ▼

British Airways has eight flights a day to Geneva with a mix of 757-200, 737-200 and A320 aircraft.

British Airways flies its 757-236s from London's Heathrow
to Geneva four times a day.

The world's most successful jetliner, the Boeing 737 was
first built for short flights and required a cockpit crew of
only two. This -300 marked a new mission and a new look.
It was 104 inches longer than the -200 model and could
carry an extra 21 passengers. A new branch of the family is
about to be born. The first member, the 737-700, will have
an even longer fuselage and greater range. The cockpit also
will be updated.

Classic Air flies two DC-3Cs powered by Pratt & Whitney
R1830-92 piston engines. They are converted C-47DLs from
1942 and 1943.

An Air Canada 747 taxis towards Runway 05. Huge here, the peaks will look smaller and smaller as they drop away during the Superjet's climbout. This airline operates a mixture of 747-100, -200 and -400 in passenger and Combi versions. The airline has ordered the Airbus A340-300 to replace its older 747s and Lockheed L-1011s. The airline no longer serves Geneva.

The DC-10-30 looked virtually identical to earlier -10 models but was powered by General Electric CF6-50 engines and had greater range. The first flight was on June 21, 1972. With Pratt & Whitney JT9D-20 engines, it was at first the DC-10-20, later changed to DC-10-40, and was first flown on Feb. 28, 1972; the first Series 40 with JT9D-59 engines flew on July 25, 1975.

▲ Britannia was the first European customer for the 737-200. It later acquired some -300s and placed orders for Boeing 767-200s and -300s.

An Aeroleasing Learjet ▶ holding for take off in front of an MD-11 near Runway 23. Geneva is an airport with much private aircraft traffic.

The DC-8 Series 62 could carry 189 passengers for 7,200 km. (4,500 miles). The DC-8 was the third of a look-alike trio of long-range, four-engine narrow-body jets, which also included the Boeing 707 and Convair 880/990. The DC-8s have had the greatest staying power, however. Many have been reengined to increase fuel efficiency and comply with newer noise rules.

Royal Jordanian flies modern A310-300s and 1970s vintage Lockheed L-1011 Tri-Stars. The newer A310s like this one have wing fences that increase lift. To extend the range of the basic A310 aircraft, the A310-300 was developed with a tailplane trim tank and optional underfloor tanks to increase fuel capacity. The A310-300 is available at maximum weights ranging from 150,000 to 164,000 kg. (330,000 to 361,600 lb.).

Both Aeroflot Soviet Airlines and the Soviet military operate the Antonov heavy-lift transport. Its four engines have sufficient power for the airlifter to have a gross weight of 362,000 kg. (800,000 lb.). The first flight of the An-124 prototype was made on Dec. 26, 1982, and production aircraft were reported to be in service by early 1986.

Tradewinds Airways of Essex, England, uses this Boeing 707-321C for freight. The aircraft is powered by four Pratt & Whitney JT3D-3B engines equipped with silencers. It was the 368th 707 made and was delivered to Pan American in 1964 with the tail-number N794PA.

This Shorts SC5 Belfast is operated by Heavylift Cargo Airlines of the UK. It owns a total of five aircraft of this type, powered by four Rolls-Royce Tyne 515-101W engines, in an all-freight configuration.

The Yak-42 can accommodate up to 120 passengers. In common with most other Soviet jet transports, the Yak-42 was designed to have a relatively high thrust-to-weight ratio, with benefit to airfield performance (including operation at high altitude airfields) albeit with some sacrifice in operating economy.

The Ilyushin Il-86 can carry 234 passengers and has a range of 2,237 km. (3,600 miles). Since its collapse, even airlines in the former Soviet Union are seeking western-built jets. Because they lacked computers capable of performing modeling with computational fluid dynamics, the Russians were unable to develop engines that matched the efficiency and durability of those built in the West.

The Tupolev Tu-134 was the Soviet answer to the Fokker F28. The medium-range jet could carry a maximum of 68 passengers. The Tu-134 had a sleeker appearance and flew faster. Six prototypes or preproduction aircraft are reported to have been used in development of the Tu-134, production of which was launched in 1964 at Kharkhov. The first production batch was followed by the appearance, in the second half of 1970, of the Tu-134A, featuring a 2.10 m. (6 ft. 10.5 in.) fuselage "stretch", providing for eight extra passengers (two seat rows) in the maximum-density, one-class layout.

Sabena recently changed its livery to that shown in the
photo. The Belgian carrier operates a mix of 737-200, -300, -
400 and -500 aircraft for its European destinations.

A Tunis Air 727-2H3 Advanced taxis past the new control tower refered to as "Goldorak". Automobiles are not uncommon sights on taxiways. They are necessary to cover the long distances on an airport, but must yield to aircraft. This airline also operates Airbus A320-211s powered by CFM56-5A1 engines to Geneva and other airports in Europe.

A privately owned 757, here on the airport west side, is a rare sight. The Boeing 757-200 maintains the same fuselage diameter as Boeing's other narrow-body aircraft, the 707, 727 and 737, but carries up to 220 passengers. Its reliable engines and new technology cockpit allow transatlantic flights.

The Canadair Challenger HL-601 is one of the world's most modern business jets. The widebody features an ultramodern glass cockpit and winglets.

▲ An Aeroleasing Learjet. The Learjeat product line has gone through a succession of owners since its founding by business jet pioneer Bill Lear. Bombardier, the Canadian conglomerate, now owns the maker of small to medium-size jets.

A rainbow arches over the rain-slicked ▶ tarmac at Geneva, the white transports looking even brighter against the forbidding sky.

A Learjet of Aeroleasing prepares for takeoff. General aviation aircraft are stored on the opposite side of the airport from the international terminal. Some can still use Geneva's original, grass strip for takeoff and landing.

It seems appropriate that REGA of Switzerland, birthplace of the Red Cross, operates this BAe 125 configured for an air ambulance role.

Speedwings operates air-taxi flights out of the airport and flies all over continental Europe and the British Isles.

The business and private tarmac on the west side of the airport has a great variety of jets. Geneva's place as a hub of international financial activity ensures that a steady stream of corporate jets fly in and out of the city.

Many United Nations organizations are based in Geneva. Jets like this Falcon 90 allow U.N. officials to quickly reach the world's hot spots in emergencies. When time is of the essence or the threat of hostilities halts commercial flights, private jets may be the only answer.

OPEC ministers frequently meet in Geneva as the cartel tries to agree on how much crude oil the members will pump from their wells. The A300-600 is the latest version of the Airbus consortium's first aircraft. The first flew on July 8, 1983, with JT9D-7R4H1 engines, and one with CF6-80C2 engines flew on Mar. 20, 1985. The A300-600R introduced in 1986 has small wingtip fences, a trimming fuel tank in the tailplane and other new internal features. The first A300-600 was delivered to Saudi Arabian Airlines on Mar. 26, 1984.

The United Arab Emirates royal aircraft fleet operates specially fitted 747SPs such as this one, as well as Boeing 707s and Airbus A300-600s, all with VIP interiors. The hump on top of the aircraft covers satellite communication equipment.

A privately owned 747SP.

▲ The leader of Qatar has at his disposal a Boeing 707 and 727. The poor fuel economy of these aircraft should be of little worry to the head of an oil-rich state. The latest purchase for its private fleet is an Airbus A340-211 powered by CFM56-5C2 engines and configured with a VIP interior.

This BAe 146-100 is part of the Queen's Flight, Elizabeth II's personal air wing. The initial variant was the BAe 146-100, providing for 82 passengers at 33 in. (84 cm.) seat pitch, or up to a maximum of 93. This has the same powerplant as the 146-200, but a maximum takeoff weight of 84,000 lb. (38,102 kg.). The 146-200, developed in parallel with the 146-100, differs only in length of fuselage and operating weights, with associated structural and system changes.

The Saudi royal family has a 747-300 at its disposal. Among the custom touches are an elevator so that members of the royal family can ascend from the ground without climbing airstairs. It also has medical facilities, including an operating room.

TEA Basle is one of the myriad charter operators serving
Geneva. Here passengers are boarding a Boeing 737-200.
The airline now operates only 737-300 aircraft powered by
CFM56-3B2 engines in a single-class 149-passenger
configuration.

U.S. President Ronald Reagan and Mikhail Gorbachev, the last president of the former Soviet Union, met in Geneva in 1985 to hammer out the details of the historic agreement that actually reduced the number of nuclear weapons in the superpowers' arsenals for the first time.

Airways International ceased operations in 1988. It operated this 737-204 from 1985 on; the aircraft was originally built for Britannia Airways and leased out to the now defunct UK operator.

G-AZUK and sister ship G-AYUW were BAC 111-475FMs operated by Mediterranean Express, a charter operator located at Luton International Airport in the UK. The carrier suspended its flights in early 1988.

Inter European Airways based in Cardiff, Wales was founded in 1986 and has configured its leased-in Boeing 737-3Y0 aircraft to carry 148 passengers in one class for its charter flights.

A U.S. Air Force C-5B, the largest western-made aircraft, is
one of the support aircraft for a presidential visit.

The presidential helicopter uses the call sign Marine One only when the chief executive is on board. The modified Sikorsky S-70 helicopter carries the special designation VH-▼ 60N.

Aircraft from the presid- ▶ ential air wing line up for takeoff on a rain-slicked runway near the cargo area.

The Caledonian Airways Lockheed L-1011-50 inbound from Gatwick is a converted L-1011-1. The UK charter operator is a division of British Airways and has a fleet of Boeing 737-200, 757-200 and L-1011-1, L-1011-100 aircraft.

Lufthansa operates Fokker 50, Boeing 737-200, -300, -400 and -500, and Airbus A320 aircraft for its flights to Geneva.

Syrian President Hafez el-Assad flew to Geneva in 1994 to meet U.S. President Bill Clinton. Assad flew on this 747SP-94, delivered during 1976, powered by Pratt & Whitney JT9D-7 engines and operated by the national airline Syrianair.

Orion Airways of Derbyshire, UK flies several Airbus A300B4-203s it acquired from Lufthansa and has them configured for charter operations in a high-density 328 passenger mode. G-BMZL was 77th off the Toulouse production line and was delivered as an A300B4-2C in 1979. The German carrier converted the aircraft to a -203 in 1983.

◀ An American Airlines 767-200 prepares to land at Geneva. Because it has extended twin-engine operations approval, the 767 is allowed to make transatlantic crossings. It may fly far enough from land that it would take 120 minutes to reach a suitable airport while flying on a single engine. No ETOPS aircraft has ever been lost over water. American no longer flies to Geneva.

▲ One of the first A320s pays a visit to Geneva during its flight test program. Operational test and evaluation flights are conducted after a plane's performance has been documented. The purpose is to "get the kinks out" before revenue service begins. The first two variants of the A320 were the A320-100 and A320-200, which have the same overall dimensions but different fuel capacities and operating weights.

Geneva Airport's new freight hall is located next to the highway. The well-known Convention Center "Palexpo" is close by.

An Antonov AN-12 turboprop aircraft, used as a freighter,
is parked near the cargo area east of the airport.

Although its capacity is limited compared with bigger jets, the BAe 146 is offered in convertible and all-freight versions. For shorter flights where they fly full, the 146 may make more sense than a larger jet with excess capacity. Certification of the BAe 146-100 was on May 20, 1983, and Dan-Air put the type into revenue service on May 27. The Series 200 was certificated in June 1983 in the U.K. and U.S., allowing Air Wisconsin to become the first operator of the type on June 27.

A Vickers Vanguard Merchantman 953C of Air Bridge of
the U.K. The aircraft is powered by four Rolls-Royce Tyne
506-10 turboprop engines in its all-freight configuration.

Federal Express's fleet ▶
on the Continent includes
this Fokker F27 turboprop.

◀ Ethiopian Airlines
operates a modern fleet
that includes this Boeing
757-200F cargo jet. It also
flies two 757s configured
for passengers, three
Boeing 767s, a 707, four
727-200s, a Boeing 737-200,
de Havilland Dash 5s and
Dash 6s, ATR-42s and two
L-100-30s, civil versions of
the Lockheed C-130.

One of the many charter operators that serves Geneva, Monarch operates Boeing 737s and larger 757s like this one. The two aircraft share a common fuselage diameter, but at 155 feet the 757 is more than 45 feet longer than the largest 737, the -400. That allows it to carry up to 61 more passengers.

An Iraqi Airways 747. Its livery accentuates the hump on this Boeing 747-200. Nearly three decades after its introduction, the 747 is still the airliner of choice for intercontinental travel. The newest version, the -400, promises to keep flying well into the 21st century.

Another charter airline, Air 2000, carries skiers bound for the Swiss Alps. Charter operators often arrange their cabins in a single class, which allows more seats and keeps fares lower for all. They typically fly at or near capacity.

Czechoslovak Airlines was among the first Eastern
European carriers to begin operating western-built
airliners like this new technology 737-500. During the Cold
War, Warsaw Pact nations could not buy or lease the
planes because of the potential military uses of technology
in their engines and avionics.

◀ Cubana is one of the few airlines in the world that still does not have access to western-built jets. Even Airbus transports, which use U.S.-developed engine technology, are off limits to the Cubans.

CSA had a dozen ▶ Ilyushin IL-62s, half of which were longer-range M versions. The engines were mounted two-abreast on either side of the rear fuselage, just like the Vickers VC-10. They carried anywhere from 122 to 186 passengers.

Its high-wing design makes the IL-76 suitable for flying from unimproved airfields. Note the windows on the underside of the nose. The prototype IL-76 first flew on March 25, 1971. The military version, featuring a tail gun turret, was under evaluation in 1974. The original unarmed IL-76 was followed by the IL-76T, which featured increased fuel in the wing center section and higher operating weights, and then by the IL-76TD, with improved D-30KP-1 engines, and further increases in fuel capacity and weights.

Record company founder Richard Branson took an unconventional approach when he transferred the Virgin Records label to his startup airline. He flew planes like this Vickers Viscount from London's Gatwick International Airport to Geneva and other destinations. Meanwhile, his initial fleet of two Boeing 747-200s successfully plied the crowded North Atlantic routes to the United States. Branson emphasized quality service and competitive pricing. One personal touch was installing high-quality sound systems so passengers could listen to his music. Though still smaller than its competition, Virgin is growing.

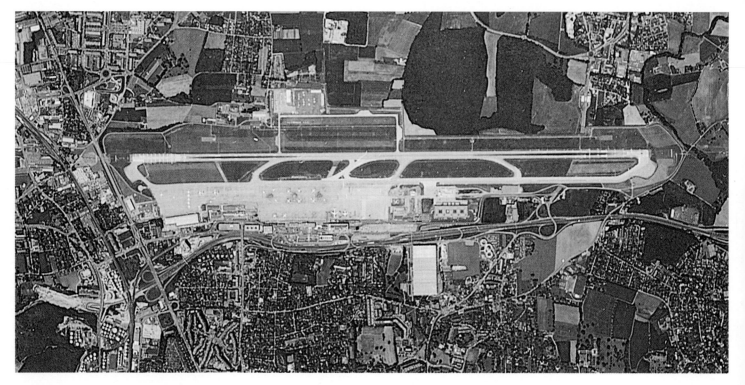

1993 Movements by Aircraft Type

McDONNELL DOUGLAS DC-9-80/MD-80	23,022	BAe JETSTREAM 31	234
BOEING 737	17,468	McDONNELL DOUGLAS DC-10	202
SAAB-FAIRCHILD 340	9,196	METRO SW 4	198
FOKKER 100	8,238	McDONNELL DOUGLAS DC-9-30	144
FOKKER 50	7,158	TUPOLEV Tu-154	172
AIRBUS A310	5,100	GULFSTREAM G2 & G3	172
ATR 42	3,762	FOKKER F28	142
BOEING 757	3,456	YAKOVLEV YAK-42	130
BAe 146	3,234	CHALLANGER CI 65 (Canadair)	112
AIRBUS A320	3,120	FOKKER F27	104
McDONNELL DOUGLAS MD-11	2,250	CARAVELLE S 210	58
McDONNELL DOUGLAS DC-9-50	1,594	McDONNELL DOUGLAS DC-3	40
BOEING 727	1,424	TUPOLEV Tu-134	38
EMBRAER EMB 120	1,116	BAC 111	34
BOEING 767	954	LOCKHEED ELECTRA L-188a	30
BOEING 747	714	McDONNELL DOUGLAS DC-8	20
LOCKHEED L-1011	674	AIRBUS A-340	18
CONVAIR 580	480	DE HAVILLAND DHC-8	10
BOEING 707	248	ILYUSHIN IL-62	8
AIRBUS A300	236	ILYUSHIN IL-76	6

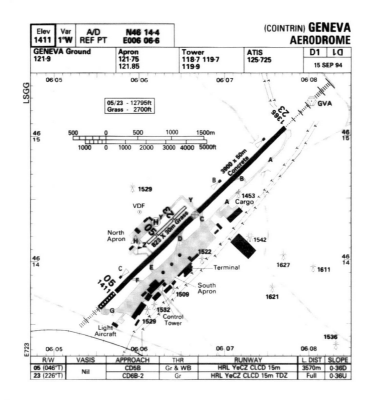

Elev 1411	Var 1°W	A/D REF PT	N46 14·4 E006 06·6		(COINTRIN) **GENEVA** **AERODROME**	
GENEVA Ground 121·9		Apron 121·75 121.85		Tower 118·7 119·7 119·9	ATIS 125·725	D1 LD1 15 SEP 94

05/23 - 12795ft
Grass - 2700ft

3900 x 50m Concrete

823 X 30m Grass

VDF

North Apron

Terminal

South Apron

Control Tower

Light Aircraft

Cargo

R/W	VASIS	APPROACH	THR	RUNWAY	L. DIST	SLOPE
05 (046°T)	Nil	CD5B	Gr & WB	HRL YeCZ CLCD 15m	3570m	0·36D
23 (226°T)		CD6B-2	Gr	HRL YeCZ CLCD 15m TDZ	Full	0·36U

General Data Geneva Airport

Airport Traffic	Passengers	Movements	Freight (tons)	Mail (tons)
1992	5,719,808	102,205	53,480	8,744
1993	5,776,119	102,599	57,182	8,135
1994	6,050,233	149,969		

Runway Data	Feet	Meters
5-23	12,795	3,900
5-23 Grass	2,700	823

Radio Frequencies	(Mhz)
Tower & Approach	118.7
	119.7
	119.9
Ground	121.9

World Airline Traffic

Year	Passenger (Millions)	Passenger km (Millions)	Tonne km (Millions)
1945	9	8,000	960
1950	31	28,000	3,490
1955	68	61,000	3,490
1960	106	109,000	12,460
1965	177	198,000	23,460
1970	383	461,000	56,690
1975	543	697,000	84,780
1980	748	1,089,000	130,980
1985	899	1,367,000	167,690
1990	1,165	1,894,000	235,240
1991	1,134	1,844,000	230,670
1992	1,156	1,933,000	241,240
1993	1,166	1,961,000	248,780